HOW TO
LAND A PLANE

MARK VANHOENACKER

Quercus

Mark Vanhoenacker, a Senior First Officer for British Airways, flies the Boeing 747 to major cities around the world. A regular contributor to the *New York Times*, he has also written for the *Financial Times*, *The Times*, *Wired*, and the *Guardian*. His first book, *Skyfaring: A Journey with a Pilot*, was a BBC Radio 4 Book of the Week. A huge international bestseller, it has been translated into a dozen languages.

Other titles in the series:

How to Play the Piano James Rhodes

How to Count to Infinity Marcus du Sautoy

How to Draw Anything Scriberia

How to Understand E=mc² Christophe Galfard

Important Notice: If you have opened this book because you find yourself in the sky, in the cockpit of a plane that you do not know how to fly, there's no need to stand on ceremony – please skip right ahead to Chapter 2, 'Aviate, Navigate, Communicate'. You can return to this introduction at a more convenient time (say, after touchdown).

Less Important Notice: I know you've got an awful lot on your plate right now and I don't wish to distract from the task at hand. But I can't help mentioning that I'm a huge fan of photographs taken from aeroplanes. Sunsets, cloudscapes, shining wings – whatever you manage to capture up there, if you think it's beautiful, then I would love to see it. Feel free to send me a picture, via the website Skyfaring.com.

Introduction

I spent a lot of my childhood dreaming of becoming a pilot. I saved my money to buy model aeroplanes, I begged my parents to take me to air shows, and whenever we flew somewhere on holiday I pressed my nose to the window with an ever-firmer love of flight. Today I'm a 43-year-old pilot of the Boeing 747. On most workdays (and work nights) I still carry a bit of that childhood joy with me across continents and oceans, above the most beautiful formations of cloud and the gathered lights of cities, under more stars than I could ever have imagined I would see.

Like many pilots, cabin crew and devoted fans of the window seat, my love for flying feels simultaneously planet-sized and deeply personal. In flight we move like mere dots through the new immensity of the sky, we see our homes so small and far below us on the unfamiliar enormity of the earth, and yet even as flying makes us feel so tiny, it uplifts us. What else does that? I'm never surprised when I hear people describe flying as an almost religious experience, nor when I encounter wings and elevated perspectives in sacred images and stories that far pre-date the Wright brothers.

For those of us who love flying, and who want to share what

we love, I think it's important to describe flight in such high-reaching terms. At least sometimes. Otherwise, whether as pilots or as passengers, we might forget how humbling and inspiring flight can be.

But there's another way to think about the wonder of flight.

We might briefly, and perhaps counter-intuitively, set aside all that soaring language (of which Exhibit A is surely the word 'soaring' itself).

We might instead approach flight through its most impersonal and mundane details, where God (or the devil, depending on which version of the expression we're using) is said to reside. We might remind ourselves that aeroplanes, like delivery vans and super-tankers and lawnmowers, are machines that people design, build and drive across the world for almost entirely practical purposes.

Re-encountering the aeroplane as 'just' a machine reminds us that flying, however remarkable, is 'just' a skill – a set of skills to be precise, that are taught, tested and regulated like any other (albeit far more rigorously than most). These skills are challenging, certainly, but they are not romantic. On the contrary, they're unusually down-to-earth. Many remain stubbornly physical, even in the most computerized modern airliner. Yet it's from these skills that the transcendence of flight is dutifully and safely assembled, many thousands of times each day.

In this short volume, I'd like to describe some of these skills – specifically, those needed to land a plane.

Why focus on the landing? While it's true that take-offs are great fun – they benefit from the exhilaration, which is to say the acceleration, that accompanies any great beginning – the landing is a better opportunity to describe a number of different skills that pilots learn. Most pilots would agree that a landing is more challenging

2

than a take-off, and it's arguably more useful (no one has to take off, after all).

It's also the case that landings, at least to me, are more momentous than take-offs. I find that's especially true when I'm flying as a passenger. I love to listen to music in the window seat, and, for as long as I can remember, it's been the landing that has demanded the best song. A landing is nothing less than how we move from the grand skies of our planet to its surface. It's how we (a flying species at last) come home.

But I promised to set aside the lofty words, didn't I? And anyway, it's almost time for you to take the controls.

Close your eyes, then, and imagine a plane high in the blue. Any plane at all (I'll try not to take it personally if you don't choose a 747).

You are going to land this plane. I hope that you'll enjoy doing so. I hope, too, that the experience will leave you with a new understanding of flight, and of why so many pilots – myself included – believe that we really do have the best job on Earth.

Before we start, a few caveats. My goal in these pages is to guide you on a flight of imagination – one that's as technically accurate as possible. Needless to say, however, this book cannot substitute in any way for professional flight training. 'I do not intend to be taken literally', wrote Squadron Leader Nigel Tangye about the title of his classic 1938 text, *Teach Yourself to Fly*. Instead I encourage – as Squadron Leader Tangye did – any sufficiently interested reader to hurry to their nearest airport, where your 'baptism of the air' may be attained for as little as five shillings (a figure that only a killjoy would adjust for inflation).

The main reason that no book can substitute for professional flight training, of course, is that flying is a physical skill you can only learn in an actual aeroplane, in the sky, with a steely-eyed instructor sitting next to you.

Another, less appreciated reason is that planes differ vastly from one another. Certain principles apply to all aircraft, of course. There's a beauty to these universals, and they are the perfect window onto both how flight works and why it's so amazing. Beyond these, though, even the more general systems and procedures that I describe won't cover *all* aircraft.

Finally, in order to focus on the fundamentals of flight during our brief time together, I've thought it best to make a few unrealistic assumptions. Sorry to say, then, that your plane has no automatic flight systems. If such wonders were to be available (they're not as easy to spot as the inflatable autopilot doll in *Airplane!*, a film that just about every pilot loves, and that you'll have a number of hopefully happy opportunities to recall in the pages to come), then you should consider jumping ahead to the 'communicate' section of Chapter 2.

Looking on the bright side, though, when you take control of your aircraft, it's cruising at an altitude that is free of tricky features in the terrain (such as mountains to fly around), adverse weather conditions and other aircraft. You are in level and unaccelerated flight, and your aircraft (aside from the aforementioned automatic flight systems) is functioning normally.

CHAPTER I

Settling In

figure 1

Hello! Welcome! Honestly, you look surprisingly calm. That's great to see.

So, this is the cockpit. Have a seat on the left – you're now the captain, after all, and that's the captain's seat. First of all, I have to ask, what do you think of the view? The world-surveying, forward-facing panorama that a cockpit offers is reason enough to become a pilot. You really are in the best seat in the house.

Fasten your seat belt, which pilots must wear whenever they are sitting down. In addition to the usual belt which goes across your lap, there may be shoulder straps or harnesses, as well as what's delicately termed a 'crotch strap'.

Now, in the spirit of a gentlemanly skipper I once flew with ('Priorities, young Mark, priorities!'), order yourself a cup of tea.

I'm joking about the tea, but only a little. One reason I prefer flying to driving is that when you're driving, whether on a busy highway or a winding country lane, if you were to let go of the wheel you'd be probably only a few seconds away from disaster. Aeroplanes are different. They are designed to be stable. If a pilot briefly took his or her hands off the controls, a plane would simply carry on doing whatever it had been doing before. For an untrained pilot, 'Do nothing' is my first bit of counsel.

So, by all means, have some tea (at the very least it will help you relax). And then, when you're ready, take a good look around the cockpit. There's almost certainly a bewildering array of buttons, levers and switches, and, depending on how modern your aircraft is, lots of digital screens. But for routine flight – including a routine landing – I promise you that a cockpit isn't as complicated as it looks.

Let's start by dividing what's in front of you into **controls** and **instruments**. To give a familiar example, in a car you can add power by using a control (the accelerator pedal), and you can monitor the result on an instrument (the speedometer). It's the same in a plane. The controls allow you to manipulate the aircraft and its systems, while the instruments give you information about the results of your inputs, as well as about the aircraft's ever-changing relationship to the outside world.

The Controls

When I was training on the 747, one of my instructors was fond of saying, 'Mark, it's just a big Cessna'. What he meant was that, while technology changes, the basics of flying don't. So, what are those basics?

A good place to start is with the famous **three axes** along which a plane can be controlled, as shown here:

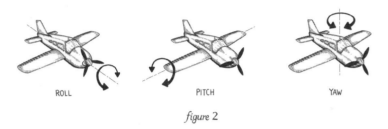

ROLL   PITCH   YAW

figure 2

Think of a line running through the nose of the plane, down the middle and out the tail. As painful as it is for me to compare the majestic 747 to a rotisserie chicken, you could imagine that the plane is on a spit. A plane can rotate from side to side along this axis. That's **roll**.

Add another line, running (roughly) between the wingtips. A plane can rotate along that axis too, tipping its nose and tail upwards or downwards, as if they were the opposite ends of a seesaw. That's **pitch**.

Finally, imagine a vertical line running through the plane from the sky to the earth. A plane can rotate around that, just as if it were on a turntable. That's **yaw**.

A pilot has controls at his or her fingertips (and toe tips) to rotate a plane along each of these three axes.

figure 3

Let's start with roll. In front of you is something that vaguely resembles the bottom half of a steering wheel. That's the **control wheel** (Figure 3). When rotated, it manoeuvres panels on the wings that essentially make one wing work better or worse than the other. The temporarily improved wing rises, the other one falls, and the aircraft rolls around its skewer-style nose-to-tail axis. From a window seat behind the wing, it's easy to see how neatly the plane rolls in response to even very small movements of the panels on the wings – a testament to how much air is flowing over them, and how fast. Rolling can also be called **banking**, and it's basically how planes turn in the sky.

Why do planes turn like this? While it's not a perfect analogy, you might think about how racetracks are often banked or inclined, especially on the curves. Indeed, some racetrack bank angles are just as steep as the bank angles typically used by a turning aircraft. (Another reason why I like the racetrack analogy: the holding patterns that planes sometimes enter when waiting to land are racetrack-shaped, with precisely drawn curves the planes must bank around...) You could also think about those little model aeroplanes you see in toy shops, which are tethered to the ceiling and race around and around in a little circle. Those planes are always turning, and always banking.

Next is pitch – the seesaw-like motion that raises or lowers the angle of the nose in relation to the horizon. Unlike a car's steering wheel, the control wheel also moves forwards and backwards on the **control column**, to which it's attached (the terms **yoke**, control wheel and control column may be used somewhat interchangeably for the combined assembly). The forward-backward motion of the control column moves either the entire horizontal part of the tail, or panels that form part of it. The horizontal part of the tail is basically a mini-wing, and manipulating it so that it works better or worse forces the tail down or up, which in turn changes the pitch (or **pitch attitude**) of the whole aircraft.

If you push forwards on the controls, the nose will lower and (in the most general terms) the aircraft will descend. Pull back, however, and the nose will rise, and the aircraft may climb. My favourite summary (which I owe to *Father Ted*, via an instructor at my Oxfordshire flight school, and which I couldn't help but quote in my first book, *Skyfaring*) is: 'Push the control column forwards, cows get bigger. Pull back, cows get smaller'.

On some planes, instead of a control wheel and column, you'll have a stick right in front of you that performs the same functions. On certain aircraft, including most Airbus jets, you'll see a sidestick controller off to one side – an incredibly expensive joystick, essentially, that processes pilot inputs in a high-tech manner that's far removed from the basics we're discussing here.

So that's roll and pitch. What about yaw? In front of your feet are **rudder pedals**. These pedals have a number of functions. Both in flight and on the ground, they control the vertical panel or panels on the tail fin of the aircraft, while on the ground the pedals are typically also used to steer the aircraft via its wheels, as well as to brake, or indeed to steer by applying the brakes. In flight the effect of the rudder pedals is to yaw, or rotate, the aircraft – again, as if it were on a turntable.

Perhaps you're wondering here why planes don't just yaw to turn, instead of rolling. Planes can indeed turn simply by yawing, but for a variety of reasons it's less effective. To go back to the racetrack analogy, if a curve wasn't banked, a car going too fast around it would skid off, right? If you simply yaw a plane, then it, too, will 'skid' in the direction it was originally travelling.

In fact, the most efficient, polished aerial turns require both banking and a bit of rudder. In a small, basic plane – the kind you might take lessons in – your instructor will drill this co-ordination of roll and yaw into you from Day One. In airliners, the co-ordination is typically automated. For today's limited purposes, on most modern aircraft, it's probably simplest to not use the rudder pedals when turning in flight. Just don't think of them as anything like the pedals in a car, which they definitely are not.

The other important control you need to find is the power.

The importance of the engine (or engines) might seem obvious. But it's a good excuse to talk about the famous **four forces** (Figure 4) that, along with the famous three axes we just discussed, are something every aspiring pilot learns about on the first day of ground school.

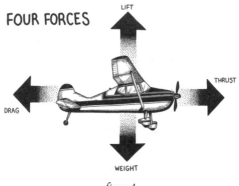

FOUR FORCES

figure 4

The plane creates **lift**, primarily from the wings. Sometimes my friends ask me how planes fly. What they usually mean is 'How does a wing work?' There are a couple of different ways of explaining it, not all of which, frankly, are very satisfying or intuitive. Perhaps the best answer is the simplest one, and that was given long ago by Wolfgang Langewiesche, one of history's greatest author-aviators. In *Stick and Rudder*, first published in 1944, he wrote: 'The wing keeps the airplane up by pushing the air down'. That venerable statement grows even more remarkable, as another pilot I know is fond of pointing out, when you see a 400-tonne 747 rise into the sky. For thousands of miles and a dozen or more hours, over deserts and mountain ranges and entire oceans, its vast, shining wings are pushing and pushing against nothing more than the invisible air.

Lift, then, primarily overcomes the **weight** of the aeroplane and of everything it's carrying into the heavens – you, your breakfast tray, this little book. It even lifts the wings themselves (which is kind of meta and best not thought about too much).

Drag is both obvious and really complicated. There are a few different kinds. But in short, drag is what you overcome when you swim, and what a plane must overcome to move through the air.

A plane overcomes drag with **thrust**, which comes from engines. (In my first days of classroom flight training, I was amazed to discover something that now seems as obvious as it is pleasing: a propeller can be thought of as a turning wing, at least in the most general sense. The best way to think about old-school jet engines, in contrast, is to imagine you're sat on a skateboard and you point something like a fire extinguisher in one direction, in order to zoom off in the opposite direction. The modern turbofan engines on airliners are a kind of clever hybrid of the two.)

Diagrams of the four forces like the one above appear in many flight training manuals. They provide a good starting point and are more than enough for today. But if you're feeling technically minded you might enjoy a more complete picture of what your aeroplane is up to:

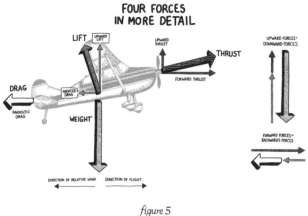

figure 5

This version adds some interesting subtleties, such as that lift itself causes some drag, and that thrust can supplement the lift provided by the wings.

But the most important thing to notice here is the horizontal arrow at the bottom that indicates the direction of flight. This plane is in level flight – even though we can see that it, and in particular its wings, are inclined slightly upwards.

Imagine that – your plane is pointing up a bit, but that doesn't mean you're going up. This fact about how planes move is probably the most important thing a pilot can share with a non-pilot. If you can't quite get a sense of how this works, there are a couple of different ways to think about it. Wolfgang Langewiesche memorably described such motion through the sky as 'mushing', which really is the perfect word for it. A friend of mine, meanwhile, is fond of the analogy with water-skiing. Your skis are inclined upwards, just like the nose and wings of an aeroplane. But your motion across the lake is horizontal – and, rather marvellously, in exactly the same way as water-skis, wings need to push on the air at a steeper angle if they're moving at a slower speed. (And just a quick aside on cool terminology – in the sky, that angle between the relative wind, or airflow, and the wing is the famous **angle of attack**.)

The diagram above is also particularly helpful in understanding that when a plane is in unaccelerated flight, the upward and downward forces, and the forward and backward forces, are balanced. When you change one of these forces, however, the system becomes temporarily unbalanced, and the plane will change direction, speed or both. When the forces stop changing the plane will find its new balance, once again in unaccelerated flight. That new balance could be a steady climb or descent, or a higher or lower speed. Or the plane could simply be pointing in a new direction. As an example, a pilot might ask the engine(s) to produce more thrust. That additional force can be used to reach a higher speed, to establish a climb, or to accomplish a mixture of the two.

Thrust, of course, comes from the engines, which leads us to the last important set of controls we need to find. Planes have different kinds and numbers of engines, and it's hard to give one rule for them all.

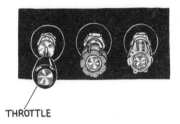

THROTTLE

figure 6

In a typical single-engine propeller plane, you will likely find a set of two or three basic engine controls for that one engine (Figure 6). The **throttle** is the most important of these. It's usually on the left, black and labelled. It may be a push-pull 'plunger'-type of mechanism, or a forward-backward lever.

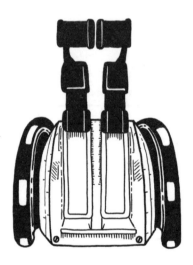

figure 7

On a multi-engine jet aircraft, such as an airliner, you'll have multiple **thrust levers** (Figure 7). Although there's one thrust lever for each engine, they're designed so that you can (and should!) move them forwards and backwards together.

So, what does moving a throttle or thrust lever do? The principle is nearly universal: forwards creates more power, backwards less. A good way to remember this is to say to yourself 'fast forward'. I've also heard it described in terms of horses – pull back on the throttle, just as you would on the reins. (Though I fear that the *Out of Africa*-esque age in which equestrian analogies were genuinely useful to new aviators is now far behind us.)

By this point, with so many controls to keep track of, you're probably wondering where you should put your hands. In general, keep one hand on the control wheel, and the other, when you're not doing something else with it, on the throttle or thrust levers. So, on most aircraft, if you're sitting in the captain's seat on the left-hand side of the cockpit, that's your left hand on the control wheel, and your right on the engine controls. (And, just to say, flying well doesn't depend on whether you're left- or right-handed. There's a reassuringly long history of co-pilots, upon promotion to captain, successfully swapping over the hands they've spent decades flying and adjusting the power with.)

So there you have it. You know how to go up and down; left and right; and faster and slower. You have basic control of the aeroplane.

The Instruments

Now let's look at the instruments. At first they may appear overwhelming. The secret, though, is to focus on what's sometimes called the 'six pack' of basic flight instruments that many generations of aviators

15

would instantly recognize (Figure 8). In fact, we'll narrow things down even further, and concentrate our efforts on four of these six – all three on the top row, plus the centre instrument on the bottom row – that make up what's sometimes called the 'basic T' or 'classic T', in reference to the shape they make. Note that in a cockpit with two side-by-side seats, each seat may have its own set of these instruments.

figure 8

The first of these four instruments to consider is the **attitude indicator** (Figure 9). Its prime position – in the centre of the top row – reflects its importance. It's also known as the **artificial horizon** (which I would point out is a far lovelier name, if I wasn't trying to focus on the non-poetic aspects of flight). The attitude indicator shows the aircraft's pitch – whether the nose of the plane is pointing upwards or downwards. This is measured in degrees (and, as we've already touched on, an upward or downward angle doesn't neces-sarily mean we are climbing or descending). Helpfully, the sky is represented as blue and the earth as brown. The line between the two represents the horizon. Indeed, in clear conditions, when you can see the actual horizon out of the window, you may hardly need this instrument to fly. In cloud, though, it's of paramount importance.

16

figure 9

The attitude indicator also shows whether the aircraft is banking, or rolling around its nose-to-tail axis. When it comes to displaying turns, the attitude indicator confuses many new pilots, who may think it shows the opposite of what it does. Take a look at the image above. Are you turning left or right? If it's not obvious to you that you're in a left turn, think about which way you'd need to roll your head (or the aeroplane that contains your head) in order to make the horizon look level. You'd need to roll to the right here in order to even things out. Ergo, you must now be banked to the left.

Perhaps the most helpful way to think about this type of artificial horizon is to remember that the displayed horizon *always* remains level with the real horizon outside. You, and your plane, simply pitch and roll around it.

figure 10

The next instrument to look out for is the **airspeed indicator** (Figure 10). It displays your speed in knots (nautical miles per hour, a unit that's just one measure of aviation's rich maritime inheritance. All the miles I refer to from now on are of the nautical type, which are about 15 percent longer than the statute miles we use on the ground.) Your indicated airspeed can be surprisingly different from your actual speed through the air, and from your speed over the ground, due to variations in air density, the effects of the wind and other factors. But all that (along with your Mach number – your speed compared to the local speed of sound, which is a whole other kettle of potentially supersonic fish) is not something to worry about today.

The important thing to take from the airspeed indicator is that you don't want to be going either too fast or too slow. But because wings only work when they're moving, too fast is definitely better than too slow. Particularly on smaller planes, you're likely to have helpful coloured zones or arcs on the airspeed indicator. Green zones and central, uncoloured zones are generally safe. Red is typically used to show maximum or minimum speeds. So avoid the red zone (in general, words to live by in aviation). On some planes, flight in the yellow zone must be avoided too. On others, it's acceptable to fly 'in the yellow' in smooth conditions. The white zone has to do with the **flaps**, which we'll come back to later on.

figure 11

Next up, as it were, is the **altimeter** (Figure 11). Air pressure falls with altitude, as your ears know very well. Much like your ears, an altimeter is sensitive to air pressure, which it translates to an elevation, usually above sea level. You read older, analogue altimeters in the same way as a clock. The hands show tens of thousands, thousands and hundreds of feet – so the altimeter in Figure 11, for example, indicates 7,000 feet. Some altimeters, not shown here, combine a set of digits with only one hand, and those are a lot easier to read.

figure 12

The fourth and final really important instrument is the **heading indicator**, or **directional gyro** (Figure 12). It displays your magnetic heading in a 360-degree format. 360 degrees is north, 90 is east, 180 is south, and 270 is west. (I know this probably isn't the best time, but did you ever wonder why there are 360 degrees in a circle? The exact details have vanished in the mists of time, but speculation centres on the Babylonians, the approximate total number of days in a year, and the fact that 360 is so neatly divisible.)

Although a heading indicator looks like and can be thought of as a compass, it's more useful. That's because a compass is subject to errors when it's turning or accelerating, both of which planes do often. On a small plane, the heading indicator must be updated by readings from the actual compass – that's what the knob on it is for – when the aircraft is in unaccelerated flight. (The various compass errors, and what they tell us about our Earth, are a source of

20

amazement to many new pilots, me included; they're a subject you may find it interesting to delve into after touchdown.)

These four instruments – the attitude, airspeed, altitude and heading indicators – form the classic 'T'.

There are two other instruments that typically appear alongside these four. At bottom left on the classic six-pack is a turn and slip indicator, the joys of which I'll leave you to discover when you take professional flight lessons. The bottom-right instrument, though, **the vertical speed indicator** (Figure 13), is worth mentioning. It does just what it says on the tin. It shows whether the plane is climbing or descending, and is typically calibrated in hundreds of feet per minute.

figure 13

Such clock-style (or analogue) instruments have been around for generations. But if you're in a newer, 'glass' cockpit, they will be

combined in something that on the Boeing 747 is called a primary
flight display (figure 14):

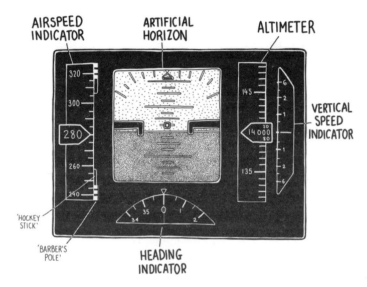

figure 14

It might look confusing. But, in fact, this screen simply gathers
together the same information as those clocky instruments of yore.
They're even in roughly the same positions as on the classic T.

At the base is a heading indicator. In the centre is a digital version
of the attitude indicator, with sky above the horizon and earth below
it. On the left is the airspeed – digits in the middle show the current
speed, while coloured bars (the 'hockey stick' and the 'barber's pole')
show various maximum and minimum speeds.

On the right is the altimeter, currently indicating 14,000 feet.

Beyond it, further to the right, is the digital version of the vertical speed indicator. The indicator line in the middle is level, as the aeroplane's altitude isn't changing. But in a descent of 1,000 feet per minute, for example, the indicator line would be angled downward, to the dash marked '1'.

(Another brief aside: the most fascinating difference between most 'clock' instruments and most 'digital' instruments isn't that some are on a computer screen. It's that, whereas on the clock-style instruments for speed or altitude, the measurements, or scale, are fixed, and the indicators move around them like clock hands, on the digital display it's the opposite. The indicator is fixed in the middle and the scale itself moves up or down behind it. When it comes to the science, and art, of displaying information, it's an entirely different philosophy. In theory, the digital version should be confusing – because, for example, the speed scale scrolls down the screen as the speed increases – but in practice it feels very natural. It's one of the features of modern cockpits that I'd love to see transplanted to mass-market cars.)

But I digress. To put it simply, these four instruments – attitude, airspeed, altitude and heading – are all you need to fly in the thickest cloud, on the darkest night.

CHAPTER 2

Aviate, Navigate, Communicate

As a professional pilot, I spend four or five days a year in multi-million-dollar flight simulators, being examined by specialized training pilots. Since professional pilots already know how to fly, much of the testing focuses on what are called 'non-normal situations' (and it's fair to say you are now in a non-normal situation).

A useful guide to your initial actions if you're in such a pickle is a simple mnemonic called ANC: Aviate, Navigate, Communicate. (Aviation is as acronym-laden a field as any I've come across.)

So, **aviate**. You need to keep the plane in the safe, stable flight you found it in.

Use the control wheel and the horizon displayed on the attitude indicator to level the wings. If it's gin-clear outside and the real horizon is obvious to you, feel free to use it.

Next, take a look at the altimeter and the vertical speed indicator. Pick an altitude as your target – a simple number near your current altitude, like 10,000 or 15,000 feet. If you're climbing away from your target, then very gently push the control column forward – that is, away from you – until you've stopped climbing. If you're descending, then pull the control column back, towards you, until you're not descending anymore. Be gentle, as it's easy to overcorrect. **Porpoising**, or repeatedly ascending above and then descending below your target altitude, is a common problem for new pilots.

Now look at the airspeed indicator. Pick a target speed toward the higher end of the safe range. It's impossible to give numbers for every aeroplane, but try 100 knots in a small plane, 250 knots in a small airliner, and 280 knots in something like a 747. If your speed is higher than your target, pull the throttles or thrust levers back slightly to reduce power. If it's lower, then add power.

The goal is to reach an equilibrium in which your speed and altitude are safe and stable. Note the pitch attitude and power setting at which this occurs. The problem, as you'll soon realize, is that the inputs required to correct one aspect of your flight path will almost certainly upset another one. For example, if you've just changed your power setting, then your pitch may have changed, and perhaps you've started to inadvertently climb or descend. Or, if you've accidentally lowered your pitch attitude, you'll soon see your speed increasing and your altitude dropping.

The best way to catch such unintended changes early is to move your eyes between the primary instruments in a consistent pattern. This pattern is called the **scan** and the scan is, unfortunately, much easier said than done, in part because it can seem repetitive at first, and in part because you must keep scanning at the same time as you're doing everything else you need to do. In fact, getting the scan right is one of the hardest parts of pilot training. It's hardly overstating it to ask you to imagine that every remaining word in this book is followed by the command 'Scan!'

Sometimes – *scan!* – just – *scan!* – maintaining – *scan!* – level – *scan!* – flight – *scan!* – requires you to hold an awful lot of forward or backward force on the controls. This brings up the important concept of **trimming**. Trimming, you might say, is a way of resetting the conditions under which the controls feel neutral. Or to put it another way, a perfectly trimmed plane would carry on doing what you want it to, even if you were to let go of the controls. It's hard to think of a good analogy from everyday life, but you could imagine a rower with one arm that's a little stronger than the other. If his boat had a rudder to steer with, he could rejig the rudder slightly to one side, so that the boat would go straight ahead without any further steering inputs, even when he was rowing as hard as he could with both arms.

Planes are typically trimmed by adjusting the positions of the panels and surfaces on the wings and tail that act on each of the three axes – roll, pitch and yaw. Imagine an engine failure on a plane that has one engine under each wing. You'd need a lot of rudder input to keep the plane flying straight ahead (think of the rower, if he stopped rowing with one arm entirely!) It's tiring to hold that rudder position for a long time – and if you trim correctly, you won't have to. In routine flight, pilots most often trim in pitch, especially after a change of speed. Look for a trim wheel, or trim switches on the control wheel. If you find you have to hold a forward force on the controls to maintain level flight, slowly roll the wheel or switches forwards until that force is no longer necessary. If you're constantly pulling back, then trim backwards. On many highly computerized jets, trimming is done automatically.

Now it's time to navigate a safe flight path (in relation to mountains, storms, air traffic zones and other aircraft) and communicate with the folks who need to know what you're doing, or who can help you to achieve a safe outcome. For a trained pilot, navigation is a more immediate priority than communication (hence the order of the mnemonic, first, A, then, N, and last of all, C). But for you the opposite is true, because unless you can see an airport right in front of you, you're going to need outside help to remain clear of terrain and to find a runway.

For that reason, we'll talk about communication first, and return to navigation afterwards. For now, if you can see mountains or other obstacles in your path, turn away from them, climb (by adding power and lifting the nose of the plane), or both.

So, **communicate**. If you haven't already put on the headset, do so now.

Radios work like a party line. Everyone tuned in to a given frequency can hear what anyone else says, but only one person can speak at a time. It's like a giant conference call in the heavens, one that can be quite intimidating for new pilots.

To speak you need to press and hold a 'Transmit' button, then release it when you've finished, just as you would on a walkie-talkie.

So, where is this button? Well, that's a good question. There's probably a button or switch on the control wheel, often on the back. If you're sitting on the left side of the cockpit then it's likely to be under your left index finger, a carefully chosen position that allows you to speak on the radio without removing your hand from the controls. Some switches rock *up* to transmit, and *down* to speak via the intercom that goes straight into the other pilot's headset (it's always a little awkward when you're eating lunch in the cockpit and you realize that you've left the intercom on, subjecting your patient colleague to a high-fidelity broadcast of every bite, chew and swallow).

You might also look for a 'hand mic', a microphone with a transmit button right on it. As you search for the transmit switch, keep in mind that on some control wheels and sidestick controllers there's an autopilot disconnect button, often red, where your thumb might land. You do not want to press that.

A pilot transmission often follows a standard four-part format: whom you're addressing (i.e., the name of the air traffic control centre; just say 'Centre' if you don't know which); who you are, expressed as a call sign, or identifier, that's absolutely unique to your aircraft or your flight; where you are; and what you want. Use your flight number or the aircraft registration (it will probably be on a placard in the cockpit) as a call sign, or choose a famous call sign from a film. *Iceman* or *Maverick*, perhaps. Give your altitude and position – as best you know it – and a concise summary of your situation. Then release the transmit button (important!) and listen for a reply.

If you don't hear one, transmit again. If you still don't hear a reply, it's time to change frequency. Look for the radio's control panel (Figure 15), which will have multiple digital displays of numbers in a certain format – typically three digits, a decimal point and then a few more digits, such as 134.975. There may be one such panel on the main dashboard in front of you, or there may be several smaller panels scattered around on the centre console (the horizontal area between the two seats).

figure 15

On each panel or panel subsection, there are typically two frequencies displayed – an active frequency on the left and a standby frequency on the right, with a ⟷ between or below them. Typically, you can only change the frequency that's displayed in the standby window. The tuning knob for the standby window has two parts – a larger outer knob, and a smaller inner one. One knob selects the digits before the decimal point, and the other the digits after it. (On newer planes, you may be able to enter the digits using a keypad.)

As no one has responded to your initial call, the frequency to enter now is 121.500 MHz, the universal emergency frequency. Select this in the standby field, then swap the standby frequency into the active field by pressing the bidirectional arrow button. Change the frequency on all the panels you can find. Also, press every radio panel button with a '1' or 'L' on or near it, to make sure you're transmitting via the correct radio, and not, for example, repeatedly making a PA (public address) to the cabin. Then transmit your call. Unless civilization as we know it has come to an end, which really would make this a very unlucky day for you, someone will answer you on this frequency.

In addition to the controller, there might be a nearby pilot who is flying the same type of aircraft as you. And, if not, the controller should be able to find one. (In the real world, of course, the first thing your new radio friends would do is help you to engage any available automatic flight systems.)

Now that you've established communications, it's time to **navigate** (Figure 16). Ask the controller for a direction to fly in to keep you clear of terrain and perhaps also bad weather – in some parts of the world the controllers can see weather systems on their screens.

You've got enough on your plate without having to deal with heavy rain and lightning bolts.

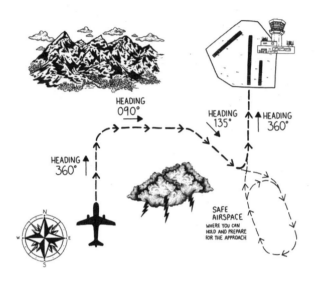

figure 16

When the controller decides that you need to turn, he or she will give you a heading (known as a 'vector'), measured in degrees, such as 090 degrees for east. Look down at the heading indicator and then gently turn the control wheel in the desired direction. You don't want to roll too steeply. Your bank angle – remember the banked racetrack if it helps – is also measured in degrees. I'd advise not rolling to an angle of more than 30 degrees (you can leave your aerobatics training for another day). On many attitude indicators, small indicator lines mark out 10 and 20 degrees of bank. The first bigger line marks 30 degrees.

Remember what I said about how each change you make to the flight path may lead to another required input? Well, here we go again. As you roll, you'll need to pull back on the control column a little and probably add power too. That's because some of the lift that was keeping you in level flight is now being deployed 'sideways' to turn you. If you don't create more lift, you'll start to descend. Pulling back creates that lift (and the more steeply you bank, the more you need to pull). But it also creates more drag, so you'll need more power to maintain your speed. And so it goes on. That's why the scan is so important.

The vectors from the controller will keep you on a safe horizontal path. As for your vertical path, if the controller tells you to climb to avoid mountains, then increase power and pull the nose gently up. When you reach your new target altitude, level out by lowering the nose and adjusting the power. To descend, it's the reverse of the climb. Reduce power, gently lower the nose and the descent follows naturally.

Now you know how to keep the aircraft flying – to **aviate**. The controller you're in communication with is helping you to navigate. In fact, you've earned a pause for another cup of tea (but actually, keep on scanning). Nor should you miss the chance to have a little fun (the technical aviation term for 'fun', by the way, is 'familiarizing yourself with the feel of the aeroplane'). Try some gentle turns or climbs or, for extra points, combine them in a climbing turn. Enjoy...

CHAPTER 3

The Best Laid Flight Plans

OK, that's enough fun. It's time for another acronym. But this one is so useful that it deserves its own chapter. It's a decision-making framework called **T-DODAR**.

T-DODAR stands for Time; Diagnosis; Options; Decide; Assign; Review. There are a number of similar frameworks in the aviation field, each with its own memorable acronym. But I like T-DODAR best because it starts with Time. I like T-DODAR so much that I sometimes use it on the ground, too. A friend of mine who has a stress-filled job in Silicon Valley has even adapted T-DODAR to help him respond to critical work situations. Whether I'm buying a new refrigerator or planning a holiday with a group of friends, T-DODAR hasn't failed me yet.

Time: As so many instructors have told me, there's almost always more time than you think there is. And it's almost always better to use more of it than you might be initially inclined to. In the sky only a few situations require instant decisions or reactions. Even one of the most critical in-flight manoeuvres − a response to a rarely heard command generated by the aircraft systems to avoid a potential collision with another aircraft − gives the pilot five entire seconds to initiate the required change to the flight path. Count them – one Mississippi, two Mississippi... – that's a long time.

So how much time do you have? In a normally functioning aircraft the main constraint will be fuel. Ask the controller for help reading the gauges that show the fuel flow to each engine and the fuel remaining in each tank – there's probably more than one. Other constraints may include the weather, both where you are and where you're going (so check, is it getting worse, or better?); the light (a first landing will be easier in daylight – when is sunset? Or dawn, if it's already dark?); and what are formally termed 'physiological needs' (at some point you'll have to think about going to the toilet).

Diagnosis: This step is more useful for professional pilots who want to review precisely which malfunction has occurred, and the reason for it, if it's known. It may help you to restate your situation out loud in clear, simple language. (And if you suspect you're dreaming all of this, perhaps as you gently doze on a plane that's taking you on a much-needed holiday, then try to wake yourself up and find something light to watch on the in-flight entertainment.)

Options: After a technical malfunction, professional pilots will talk through potential courses of action, being sure to account for the possibility of further problems. For example, if one of the pumps in one of the 747's many fuel tanks has failed, what happens if a second one fails before landing?

The main question for you to settle right now is where to land. The chances are that you'll have enough fuel to reach a number of different airports. Ideally, one of them will offer:

- A nice, long runway. The longer the better. At least 1,500 metres long if you're in a small plane, or 2,500 metres if you're in an airliner

- A lighting system called PAPIs (Precision Approach Path Indicators)
- No significant terrain or obstacles nearby
- Dry conditions and good visibility, under either clear skies or a very high cloud base – say, at least 5,000 feet up – with no en route severe weather or icy conditions
- Favourable winds on the runway (headwinds, a synonym for adversity in everyday life, are in fact a big help for landing, and for take-off, too, because they reduce the amount of runway you'll use)

A great many airports will meet the first three requirements.

Decide: In your situation the controller (who may be a pilot as well) will have the best idea of where you should land. But for better or worse, it's your call. It's your 'ship now' – you're 'in charge...the boss...top dog, big cheese, the head honcho...'

Assign: (the tasks). This is really important in an airliner that has two or more pilots, not to mention cabin crew and on-call engineering experts on the ground. But it's relevant to your situation too. Outsource what you can to the controller, and be clear about what you don't have the time or spare mental capacity to do. If there's someone else on board, then let them work the radio while you concentrate on the flying (which is exactly how tasks are typically divided on a two-crew aircraft).

Review: This is just like the continual scan of the instruments. But instead, you're scanning your situation. Are the controller's transmissions becoming garbled as you fly further away? Is your fuel ticking down at roughly the rate you'd expect? Jump back to the start of T-DODAR to handle any unexpected changes.

CHAPTER 4

Preparing for the Approach

Once you've chosen an airfield and runway, tell the controller that if possible you want – trust me on this one for now – a 25-mile, straight-in approach, with a descent starting 3,000 feet above the airfield.

Say that you'd like to proceed to the vicinity of the airport but that you don't necessarily want to land right away. As long as you have enough fuel, pretty much the worst thing you can do is rush into an approach before you're ready. If you get to your destination with time to spare, the controller can give you a series of further vectors to keep you nearby, in safe airspace. Ideally, start the approach when you have at least one hour's fuel remaining. Set a timer or ask the controller to do so.

Now use whatever spare time that leaves you to accomplish or rehearse some important pre-landing tasks.

Let's start with the altimeters. A plane whose altimeters say it's at 35,000 feet may in fact be quite a bit higher or lower than 35,000 feet. After all, an altimeter is only an air-pressure sensor, and air pressure varies with weather, time and location.

At high altitude, it makes sense to set aside these local variations, and so pilots set their altimeters to a kind of global average of air pressure. At lower altitudes, in contrast, we need to know precisely how high we are. So we tune the altimeters to a local, very recent measure of air pressure, using a knob that's typically on or near the altimeter itself. The controller will give you the current pressure setting at your destination. When you change the pressure setting, your altitude will appear to change, too, even though you haven't climbed or descended. To quote my brother: 'It's some pretty crazy sh*t'. (At a quieter moment, you can follow a link on my website to a *New York Times* excerpt from my first book that explains this phenomenon in more detail.)

Before you start the approach, it's also worth thinking about exactly how, later on, you'll slow down for landing. The slower you're going, the less runway you'll use. Fly too slowly, however, and you won't get enough lift from the wings. It's too late to add on bigger wings, of course, so the next best thing is to extend panels called **flaps** (and similar devices called **slats**, but don't worry about the difference) from the wings you already have (figure 17):

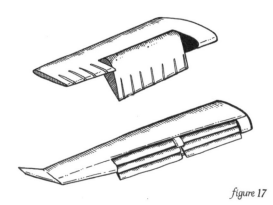

figure 17

Flaps expand a wing, change its shape, or both. When you fly on an airliner, you might notice the engines briefly getting quieter during the approach, followed by the whirring of the flaps as they are extended. That's a good indication that you're slowing down for landing. (Next, you'll typically hear the engine noise rise again, as the pilots add power to maintain the new, lower speed.) Easy to spot from a window seat, flaps on airliners can be incredibly complex. I was utterly transfixed by them as a child. They seemed to be a highly technical but also joyful kind of expansion, a wing-spreading that to a ten-year-old, at least, was something like that of a bird.

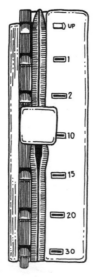

figure 18

On most large planes the flap lever (Figure 18) is typically located on the centre console, often to the right of the thrust levers. Or there might be a toggle switch, or a moveable bar between the seats that looks something like a car's handbrake. The settings are measured in degrees, such as 5, 10, 20, or in simplified settings like 1, 2, 3 and FULL.

Generally speaking, flaps allow you to fly more slowly – just what we want for landing. They also reduce your maximum safe speed – think of it as your speed limit – which makes sense if you think of the force the flaps must absorb as they're lowered further and further into all that fast-flowing air. On those planes that have a digital airspeed indicator, the coloured zones that mark your maximum and minimum speeds should automatically move to reflect the limits for each new flap setting. Stay a good 10 knots above the minimum speed that's typically marked in yellow. Keep in mind that, in order to lower the flaps to the next setting, you'll need to be already below the maximum speed for that new setting. The maximum speed for each setting is usually displayed on a sign in the cockpit.

On many planes with a clock-style airspeed indicator, flap speeds are more straightforward. On the airspeed indicator (have a look back at Figure 10 on page 18) you'll see a white arc. The top (or highest) speed on that arc is the speed you must be below in order to lower the flaps for landing. The bottom (or lowest) speed on the white arc – which is lower than the bottom on the green arc, your previous minimum speed – becomes your new lowest safe speed once the flaps are extended.

Before you start the approach, make sure you also know how to find the landing-gear lever (Figure 19). If there is one, that is – some planes don't have retractable landing gear. Look for a lever on the main console that might look as if it has a wheel on the end (coincidence? No.) Like the flaps, the landing gear has a maximum speed, usually posted near the lever or on the same panel as the flap speeds. A friend of mine finds it almost unbelievable that the lowering of

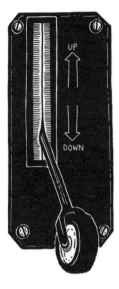

figure 19

the landing gear – a *Nutcracker*-calibre choreography of wheels (18 of them on a 747), the many panels that need to move out of their way, and all sorts of controls, sequencers, position sensors and locking mechanisms – is controlled by just one large and ridiculously simple switch. I agree.

Next, depending on how much time you have, and your type of aircraft, the controller (assisted, perhaps, by other pilots) may talk you through some further adjustments you need either to make now, or be poised to make later. It's impossible to cover all the options here, but they might include the fuel-and-air **mixture control**, the carburettor heat, the alternate air, the propeller control, fuel tank and pump selections, anti-icing systems, as well as a number of settings that will help you slow down after you land: **reverse thrust** to redirect the power of the engines, **autobrakes** to automatically engage a preselected level of wheel braking, and **speedbrakes** to automatically deploy panels on the wings that will help lower the plane's weight onto the wheels.

Finally, some tidying up (we're professional aviators, after all, not Neanderthals, who, we must remember, never learned to fly). Clear away the empty cups of tea and anything else in the flight deck that's not tied down. Make sure you can reach all the controls easily, including the rudder pedals, which you'll soon need. Get your Aviator sunglasses ready if you think you'll be landing into low sun (or if you just want to look timelessly stylish). And, while it may sound obvious, now is the perfect time to adjust your seat height and check that you can, in fact, see over the dashboard.

CHAPTER 5

Here We Go, or, 'I Just Want to Tell You Both, Good Luck. We're All Counting On You'

For trained pilots, each phase of a flight has its own formalized briefing (an advance discussion between the pilots about what they're going to do next, and how). Each phase also has a checklist to confirm that essential items are completed.

For now, let's concentrate on another mnemonic that comes up on every approach briefing, but that is especially pertinent for a landing in an abnormal situation: the famous **five stages** (no, not denial, anger, etc.) These are the **initial approach**; the **final approach**; then maybe a **go-around** – a routine manoeuvre in which you break off an approach, climb away, and come back to start the procedure again – followed by, at last, the **landing** and the **taxi-in** to the parking position.

We'll dispense with the fifth stage, the taxi-in, because you can just stop the plane on the runway and learn how to drive it along the ground another day. We will also set aside the go-around, which is most often required when an aircraft landing ahead of you takes longer than expected to vacate the runway – a situation that the air traffic controllers will be certain not to put you in today. That leaves us with three stages to work through: the initial approach, the final approach, and the landing.

I can't begin to count the number of times that an instructor has told me that 'a good landing comes from a good approach'. But what is an approach, exactly? And how do you fly a good one?

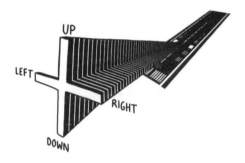

figure 20

Imagine a brave fellow standing on your intended runway, carefully aiming an optical instrument up into the sky at a shallow angle. Now imagine the crosshairs in that instrument, as if you could see them as bars of light projecting out of the instrument, and expanding as they move out and up into the sky (Figure 20). We'll call those crosshairs the **glidepath** (that term also has a more technical meaning, which we'll set aside for now). The purpose of an approach is to get onto the glidepath while still some distance away from the airport, and then to follow it right down to the runway.

LEFT/RIGHT ALIGNMENT

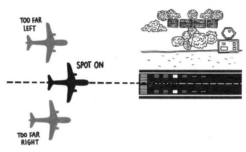

figure 21

Instead of crosshairs, you could also think of the glidepath as a set of imaginary railway lines sloping from high in the sky all the way down to the runway. But the image of the crosshairs is the better one, I think, because it makes it clear that your left-to-right alignment (Figure 21) and your vertical alignment (Figure 22) are two different tasks.

VERTICAL ALIGNMENT

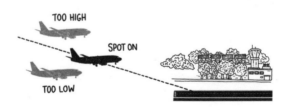

figure 22

Left-right (or lateral) navigation is pretty straightforward. Vertical navigation is a little more complicated, so let's take a more detailed look at how it works, and run through some of the specialized terminology associated with it.

VERTICAL ALIGNMENT
IN MORE DETAIL

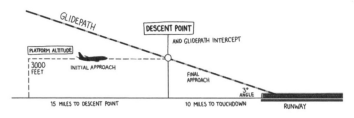

figure 23

The typical angle between the glidepath and the ground is three degrees. Roughly 10 miles away from the runway, a three-degree glidepath will have risen around 3,000 feet, and, of course, from there it continues to rise as you go even further away from the runway. We'll call that height of around 3,000 feet your **platform altitude** (it's also called an **initial approach altitude**, but the term 'platform' is more descriptive, I think). We'll call the approximately 10-mile point at which the glidepath crosses this altitude your **descent point**.

We're almost ready to delve into the individual steps of the approach. But before we do, here's an executive summary (or what actual executives, in the business world, might call the '35,000 foot takeaway'). You're going to focus on your left-right alignment first, and worry about the vertical element later. To do this, you're going to descend towards your platform altitude and then simply fly level there, turning left or right until you're flying directly underneath the glidepath and towards the runway. Then, as you intercept the glidepath – that is, as you reach the descent point of 3,000 feet upon it – you'll gently add in the vertical aspect of the approach as you start to descend along the glidepath's downward-angled slope. From then on, you'll follow the glidepath, in both the left-right and vertical senses, all the way down to the runway. Ready? Here we go.

The Initial Approach

Descend now to your platform altitude. Keep in mind that if your destination is 700 feet above sea level, say, then your platform altitude will be 3,700 feet. Level out at the platform altitude and make sure you regularly scan your speed and altitude as you move through the next steps.

Now picture the glidepath – the crosshairs that slope down through the sky to the runway. At 25 miles out and only 3,000 feet up, you won't have intercepted the glidepath yet; it's still quite far above you, and it's also somewhere off to your left or right.

Of course, you can't actually see the glidepath. Nor are you likely to be able to see the runway itself yet. So, the controller will give you a series of headings to bring you in underneath the glidepath. Since you're starting this process 25 miles out, and your descent point is at around 10 miles, you've got 15 miles to nail your left-right alignment. Fifteen may sound a lot – think of a town 15 miles away from your home – but in a speedy jet those miles will go by very quickly indeed. (In a slower plane, it would be quite reasonable to start the approach closer in.) Whatever kind of plane you're in, it's never too early to slow down. Deploy the first few stages of the

flaps, reducing to your new target speed after each stage. Be prepared
to adjust the pitch, the power, and the trim.

This is also the time to start looking out of the windows for the
runway. Turn on all the landing lights – the switches are likely to be
on the overhead panel right above the windscreen, or on the main
dashboard. Have a look around for the windscreen-wiper switches,
too, in case you need them later on.

There's no hard-and-fast rule as to when you'll be able to see
the runway. It depends a lot on the weather and the time of day. In
general, though, runways always look much smaller than you think
they will. The planet is an awfully big place, and the angle you're
coming in at makes the runways on it look smaller still. And if you're
landing at night? Most of us think of airports as quite well-lit places,
and it's true that the apron areas around the terminal buildings are
often brightly illuminated. But taxiways and runways are so subtly
lit that picking out an airfield at night, especially in an urban land-
scape, often involves looking for a particularly dark spot. Closer
in, thankfully, the approach and runway lights are unmistakable.

Once you can see the runway, tell the controllers you are 'visual'.
You no longer need their vectors to line yourself up underneath
the glidepath. You know for yourself that you're underneath it
because you can see that you're moving towards the runway along its
extended centre-line. From this point on, your left-right manoeuv-
ring will be no different than driving a car on a wide road towards a
narrow, one-lane bridge, say, or, indeed, than pulling into a garage,
except that you might be doing it at something like 160 knots.

In fact, your left-right alignment will require vigilant monitoring
and constant adjustments for the rest of the flight. If you continually
have to correct your alignment in one particular direction, then it's
likely that you're struggling with a crosswind. Do you remember

those maths problems in school in which you had to calculate the correct angle to go straight across a swiftly flowing river? That's similar to what you have to do now. Pointing the aircraft slightly into the wind should allow you to fly straight down the line that leads to the centre-line of the runway. The task is complicated, though, by the fact that both the strength and the direction of the wind are likely to change as you descend.

The Final Approach

Now that you've sorted your left-right alignment (though again, it's something to watch constantly), you need to work on your vertical alignment. Unfortunately, this part is harder. At this point the glidepath is still above you, so you need to stay at 3,000 feet until the glidepath crosses through your altitude at the descent point, about 10 miles from touchdown.

It's often difficult to judge when you meet the glidepath. Indeed, it can be hard to know exactly when you are 10 miles away from the runway. Even a professional pilot will often use the flight computers or various kinds of radio navigation aids to help gauge when to 'start down'. The controller can look at a radar display and tell you where you are in relation to the descent point. They can also tell you what you might see on the ground – a motorway, a prominent hill, a golf course – as you near it.

As you reach that point – i.e., as you at last intersect the glidepath that is steadily descending from above you – carefully lower the nose of the plane and reduce power to start your descent along it. Use the vertical speed indicator to help set a vertical speed that allows you to descend exactly with the crosshairs.

And what is the right vertical speed? It depends on how fast you're going over the ground. Imagine you're going down a staircase – the faster you're going forwards, the faster downwards you have to go also in order to stay on that invisible slope. Pilots learn some useful numerical shorthand methods to calculate or check various figures when they're up in the sky, and there's an easy one for working out your descent rate. Divide your ground speed – it's different from your airspeed, and will appear on the controller's screens, and possibly on your cockpit screens as well – by two, and add a zero to that to get the answer. For example, with a ground speed of 150 knots you need a descent rate of 750 feet per minute.

By now you're probably thinking, 'Wouldn't this be a lot easier if I could actually *see* the glidepath?' Indeed, it would, and when you first contacted the controllers, you asked them to find you a runway equipped with PAPIs, or Precision Approach Path Indicators (see figure 24 below). These red-and-white angled lights, placed in the grass or pavement off to the side of the runway, don't show you the glidepath itself. But they do show your relationship to it.

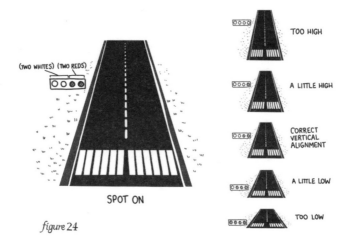

figure 24

The typical PAPI setup at major airports has four lights (or groups of lights). If you can see four white lights, then you're flying much higher than the glidepath. Four reds mean you're far too low (and if you spot a runway's PAPIs while driving past on a nearby road, four reds is exactly what you'll see). Three whites indicate that you are slightly above the glidepath, and three reds that you're slightly below it. There are other versions of PAPIs, with different names and configurations, but the principle is the same – whites are high, reds are low.

With PAPIs, two reds and two whites is perfect – indeed, I've even heard pilots use this in non-aviation contexts. 'How are things going, Jane? All set for Christmas?' 'Yeah, not bad. Two reds, two whites.' In general, if you can see some of each colour, then things could be worse.

On a clear night, you may even be able to see the PAPIs *before* you get to the descent point – great stuff, if so. Flying level at 3,000 feet, you'll know you're nearing the descent point when the PAPIs start to change from four reds (because you're intercepting the glidepath from below it) to a mixture of white and red.

If you must land on a runway without PAPIs, it really isn't your day. But if that's the case, a good alternative technique for judging your approach path is to adjust your altitude and descent rate to make sure the runway doesn't move up or down in the cockpit window at all. (A scratch or a squished bug on the windscreen can be helpful in monitoring this.) In fact, this is how student pilots are typically taught to fly an approach, precisely because it's so basic.

Even with PAPIs, though, the final approach is challenging for new pilots. The most common problem is porpoising above and below the glidepath. Watch the PAPIs like a hawk (if hawks needed PAPIs, which they probably don't) and react as soon as you see any indication that you're getting too high or too low. As soon as you see three reds, for example, gently reduce your descent rate. Don't wait until you see four.

Early corrections make it easier to follow another piece of advice that student pilots hear often: fly gently. It's often said, even – or especially – by senior pilots, that 'the plane knows how to fly better than you do'. Think of your job as applying 'pressure' one way or the other, rather than making big, wholesale movements of the controls.

A question I often hear at this point in a flight-simulator ride is, 'Where should I be looking?' The answer is 'Outside, more and more'. First to find the runway and PAPIs, then to follow them (remember, PAPIs don't help with your left-right alignment, which you must judge by looking at the runway). But, simultaneously, you'll need to maintain your scan of the instruments, particularly of the airspeed indicator, because this is pretty much the worst possible time to find yourself flying too slowly. Try thinking of the PAPIs and the runway as new, additional instruments, ones that just happen to be located a few miles beyond the others.

Amidst all this scanning, don't forget to put the aircraft into its correct configuration for landing. In an airliner, lower the landing gear when you're around 2,000 feet above the airfield. As you move the lever to 'Down', be prepared to add power, because the landing gear greatly increases drag (indeed, lowering the gear is a sure-fire way to quickly reduce your speed). Once it's completely down – it can take a while to get there on a large plane – deploy the remaining flaps and reduce to your final approach speed. It's OK if you've forgotten about those rudder pedals. But now, make sure your feet are up against them.

Next, complete the landing checklist, which, on most airliners, is used to carefully confirm that the speedbrake is armed for touchdown, the gear and flaps are correctly positioned, and the cabin is ready (you know the drill – seats upright, seatbelts fastened, hand baggage stowed, etc.) for landing.

At some point the controller will give you a formal landing clearance, a pleasing bit of technical jargon which still sounds as cool to me as it ever did: 'Awesomeness Flight 101,' – or whatever call sign you chose – 'you are cleared to land on Runway 36.'

The Landing

Let's talk through the last 1,000 feet of your flight.

Remember when Luke Skywalker says he's not afraid, and Yoda says, rather ominously, 'You will be'? And then he repeats it, even more ominously? Needless to say, such comments are not considered best practice among professional flight instructors. But it's quite natural to be a little nervous right now. Even the most experienced pilots once had to do a first landing, and you can bet they were nervous too. The margins for error become ever smaller as you get closer to the runway, and you have less time (and space) to recover from any unwanted loss of speed or altitude.

Even so, this is often one of the quietest times in the cockpit (aside from loud automated announcements, such as the memorable command, heard upon reaching the altitude at which the pilots must be able to see enough to continue the approach visually, to 'Decide!'). The checklists, the radio calls, and the major changes to the aircraft systems are mostly complete. From here on in, it's just about the flying.

At 1,000 Feet

If you watch planes in the last minute or two before landing, it's remarkable just how steady they appear. Even on windy days they can look as if they're simply hanging in the air or gliding down a perfectly smooth set of rails in the sky. That's because their approaches are stable, and now's the time to check that yours is too. On airliners like the 747 we formally check the stability of the approach 1,000 feet above the ground (a height that would be considered unnecessarily conservative in a light aircraft). Is the landing gear down, and are the flaps in the planned landing position? Is the plane on the glidepath – i.e., steady at the centre of the imaginary crosshairs, not swinging above and then below it? Do you have two reds, two whites on the PAPIs? And is your speed appropriate, not too fast and certainly not too slow?

If you meet the stable-approach criteria, then you can continue to descend. If not – or if a once-stable approach becomes unstable at any point before landing – break off the approach and try again.

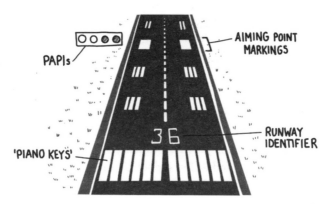

figure 25

At 500 Feet

Take a good look at the markings on the runway itself (Figure 25). The altitude at which they'll become clear to you depends on the time of day and the weather. Don't aim for the start of the runway, where the black and white 'piano key' stripes are located – on a big plane the landing gear can be 30 metres behind the cockpit, and there are carefully prescribed buffers built into both the beginning and the end of the landing manoeuvre. Instead, near the PAPIs, you'll see some blocky, solid markings, usually two solid white rectangles. These are called aiming points. So, as the name suggests, aim for these. Or just keep following the PAPIs – two red, two whites! – which will generally guide you to an acceptable touchdown position.

At 200 Feet

Somewhere in the last few hundred feet, especially in a large plane, the aircraft may start to 'float' above the glidepath. For example, you might suddenly see that you have three whites and one red on the PAPIs.

This is called the **ground effect** and it's caused by the plane compressing the air underneath its wings, which, we might say, can no longer get out of the way as the wing gets ever closer to the ground. This cushioning effect sounds pleasant, even helpful. But it's neither, because the higher you are at this stage, the farther along the runway you'll probably touch down. A gentle forward press on the controls and a tiny reduction of power will help you fly through the ground effect.

At 100 Feet

From 100 feet up, if you did nothing else but fly the aeroplane right down onto the runway, the result would most probably be an extremely firm touchdown, and an awful lot of smoke from the tyres when your landing appears on the evening news. But the plane, and you, would fly again.

Still, let's aim for something a little more refined. The landing manoeuvre starts with the **flare**. Techniques vary, but usually, when you flare, you pull the nose of the plane up a little while starting to reduce power. Raising the nose reduces the descent rate, allowing you to lightly descend onto the runway.

The flare is a tough manoeuvre and it's one that pilots continue to refine throughout their careers. Birds, unsurprisingly, can show us how it's done. A pilot friend of mine is particularly keen on watching seagulls flare just before they touch down on a beach. Otherwise, various (human) instructors over the years have given me several useful pointers.

The main challenge of the flare is knowing when to start it. On an airliner, the height at which the flare is initiated might be 30 feet or higher – that's the height of the top of a three-storey building! In a smaller plane, with a lower vertical speed and with less momentum to act against, the flare may take place closer to the ground. (When a former colleague of mine first learned to fly – on a Tiger Moth biplane, in the summer of 1959 – his instructor told him to 'keep going down until you can see the blades of grass.')

That leads nicely to a second bit of sound advice: the flare is judged visually. By the time you prepare to perform the flare – confident that you're at the correct airspeed, having scanned throughout the final approach – you should be looking almost exclusively outside.

And where exactly should you look to judge the flare? Certainly, not straight down. On many aircraft, the common advice is to look towards the far end of the runway for the last 100 feet or so of flight. This is the best way to finesse your left-right alignment, and also to assess your pitch attitude just before you start to change it. Your peripheral vision and the overall sense it gives you of the ground rising up around you will help you judge your height and your vertical speed.

A final pointer I can offer, from my experience of the airliners I've flown, is to remember that raising the nose is not a continual process. When I take guests into the flight simulator, they may start the flare at just the right time. But they often continue to pull the nose of the plane up, which results in a brief, additional and unin-tended flight – aptly called **ballooning** – followed by a memorably sharp touchdown. Instead, pull the nose up a little, start to reduce power, and then hold the nose exactly where it is. (On some planes, especially small ones, you may learn to pull the nose up continuously at this point, essentially stalling the plane. But – for a first go – the above technique is probably best).

As you flare you also need (finally!) to think about the rudder pedals. If you're landing in a crosswind, the plane's wheels won't be pointing in the direction you're moving in. Awkward! If this is the case, gently squeeze the left or right rudder pedal to sweep the nose of the plane around so that it lines up with the runway. And those unintended consequences I mentioned? On some aircraft, as you bring the nose around, one wing may start to rise, and the other to dip. Use the control wheel to keep the wings level.

Touchdown – sweet, sweet touchdown – will occur shortly, by which point, on most planes, the power should be at its minimum, or idle, setting. If touchdown doesn't occur within a few seconds, well, then that's a **float**, and it means you're unnecessarily and all too rapidly using up the remaining runway. Immediately relax any backward pressure on the control column to re-establish a shallow descent.

Most aircraft are designed to touch down on their main wheels first, followed shortly after by the nose wheel (or wheels). But even after all the wheels are on the ground, hold off on giving yourself that pat on the back, because you've still got some work to do. Perhaps my most vivid experience of flight training was the realization that a plane travelling at high speed on the ground, whether just before take-off or just after landing, is basically flying along the surface of the Earth. Even after touchdown, gusts of wind will act upon the plane, and you need to rely mostly on the controls that act on the passing air to direct the aircraft's course along the ground. You're not driving yet!

Select the engines to reverse (if they have a reverse mode). The autobrakes, if fitted and armed, will bring the plane to a complete stop. Otherwise, on nearly all planes you need to use your toes to push down on the tops of both rudder pedals to brake, while simultaneously using the whole of the pedals to steer the plane along the runway. Thankfully, this is more intuitive than it sounds. Remember, however, that on the ground you must never use the control wheel to try to turn left or right, as if the control wheel were a car's steering wheel. The control wheel rolls the plane from side to side along its nose-to-tail axis, and, on many planes, too much roll near the ground could result in a wingtip or an engine striking the runway.

As the plane slows, it inevitably – and rather sadly – starts to act less like the grand celestial conveyance it is and more like an awkward, very expensive car. As you come to taxiing speed, bring the engines out of reverse, stop the aircraft with the pedal brakes and then apply the **parking brake**. This last item is usually fitted to the central console. In order to engage it, you may need to simultaneously hold the pedal brakes fully forward.

And…Breathe

figure 26

That's it! Wipe your brow, unpeel your clenched fingers from the control wheel one by one, and change your underwear as needed. And if it wasn't the gentlest landing in history, take heart. Every pilot remembers very well what every instructor hammers into us: a good landing is one that occurs *in the right place and at the right speed*. A firm touchdown is, if anything, preferable to a softer one if the runway is short, wet or snow-covered, or if it's very windy. As it says in the fine print of the mighty 747's manuals: 'A smooth touchdown is not the criterion for a safe landing.'

By now someone should be driving the disembarkation steps, a magnum of champagne and a big medal for you to the side of the aircraft. Before they arrive, you'll want to shut off the engines. In general, on a small propeller plane, start by pulling back the red mixture-control knob (near the black throttle) all the way towards you. On other planes, look for **fuel control** or **engine master** switches, which will generally be found just behind the thrust levers on the centre console. Move them (or any other engine-control knobs, switches or levers you can find) back to the off or **cut-off** position. You may need to pull them out to do so as, for obvious reasons, they're designed to be hard to move.

Lastly, if you're on an airliner, you'll need to disarm the escape slides attached to the doors. If you've still got your headset on, press the PA button on the audio console, pause for effect, and announce: 'Cabin crew, doors to manual and cross-check.' Then grab your cap, take a selfie or two, give the control wheel a final affectionate pat and head out onto the waiting Earth.

ACKNOWLEDGEMENTS

I am very grateful to my colleagues and my instructors, far too numerous to name here, who over the years have shared their insights and experience with me, and who have answered my questions and pointed me to better ones, and who, day in and day out, make the job so rewarding.

I am also very grateful to my editor, Katy Follain, for all her kind guidance throughout this project; to her colleagues Natasha Hodgson, Charlotte Fry, Georgina Difford, Melanie Thompson, Elizabeth Masters and Olivia Mead; to my agents, Caroline Michel and Tessa David of Peters, Fraser and Dunlop; and to Amber Anderson, without whose wonderful illustrations it would be all but impossible to share many of the things I find most fascinating about flight.

This book also benefitted enormously from family members, friends, and more or less perfect strangers who responded kindly when I reached out for help. I would like to express my deep gratitude to Mark R. Jones, Kirun Kapur, Steven Hillion, Andrew Blum, Tony Cane, Lindsay Craig, Robert Goyer, Terry Kraus, Mac McClellan, Harriet Powney, Lizzie Seetharaman, Sebastien Stouffs, and Tom Zoellner.

For technical assistance I am particularly grateful to two kind former colleagues, Alex Fisher and Philip Hogge; to the fighter pilot, test pilot, and airline pilot Chris Habig; to the writer and pilot-of-all-trades Bill Cox; to Mark Feuerstein; to a former instructor, Steve Rees, from whom I expect I will always have a great deal to learn; and to Jennifer Inman and Matthew Inman, who once again offered me warm-hearted advice and brilliant technical feedback. It was Jennifer's idea to include a second, more detailed version of the 'four forces' diagram, and Figure 5, on page 12, is based on a drawing that she made for me.

Any errors of fact or interpretation are, of course, my responsibility entirely.

London, June 2017

First published in Great Britain in 2017 by

Quercus Editions Ltd
Carmelite House
50 Victoria Embankment
London EC4Y 0DZ

An Hachette UK company

A CIP catalogue record for this book is available from the British Library

ISBN 978 1 78648 715 5

Jacket design by Setanta, www.setanta.es
Jacket illustration by David de las Heras
Illustrations by Amber Anderson

10 9 8 7 6 5 4 3 2 1

Text designed and typeset by CC Book Production

Printed and bound in Great Britain by Clays Ltd, St Ives plc